Great Granny Chan

Written and illustrated by Sue Cheung

Collins

Great Granny Chan had hardly opened the car door when a boy ran out of the house shouting, "She's here!"

His brother and mum came rushing out too. His dad emerged from the driver's seat and announced, "Meet your Great Granny Chan. You can call her Granny!"

It was the first time she'd met her family in England.

"*Ni hao*," Granny said.

"That means *hello*, in Chinese," said Dad.

Dad, or Li as he was called, was the only one in the family who could speak Chinese. Granny knew just a few English words, so it was useful to have him to translate.

"This is Jack who's ten, Luke who's eight, and my wife Anna," said Li, in Chinese.

"Hello, Granny," they replied, helping her out of the car like she was a delicate little doll. Granny was perfectly capable, but they weren't to know.

They escorted her into the lounge and sat her down.
But Granny wasn't tired; she was raring to see this
new country. Not wanting to appear rude, she smiled
and drank her tea.

"Pppfff!" she spluttered. "We don't put milk in our tea
in China!"

"Sorry, I forgot!" said Li.

He explained what they were saying to the family, and
everyone laughed.

"Ask Granny what else is different in China," said Jack.

"Yeah, what's it like over there?" said Luke.

"Let her settle in before you start asking questions," Li replied. "She's 90 years old, remember."

Granny had no idea what they were saying, but the kids sighed loudly.

Whilst Anna made dinner, Li got out a jigsaw puzzle. He was being thoughtful, but to Granny it was pretty boring. She could tell the kids weren't interested either. The picture on the box showed people shearing through frothy waves on a sailing boat. She'd much rather have been doing that.

At dinner time, the doorbell rang. It was their neighbour Mr Perry, who was 82 and lived on his own. He came round every week for a meal and some company.

"You must be Great Granny Chan!" he said, shaking her hand vigorously. He was tall, thin and lively for his age, like Granny.

"*Ni hao,*" she said.

"That means *hello*, in Chinese," said Luke. "Granny doesn't speak much English."

Anna handed out plates of food and everyone tucked in, but Granny wasn't used to the knife and fork and they kept slipping about in her fingers.

"Are you having problems?" asked Li.

Granny thought for a moment, then pulled out a pair of chopsticks from a collection in her handbag. "From China!" she replied triumphantly.

Mr Perry chuckled. "Can I try?" he asked, pointing to Granny's chopsticks and then to himself.

How hilarious that he should want a go, thought Granny, so she gave him a pair, and then the kids wanted to try too. Dinner certainly livened up after that, especially when they tried to eat their peas!

The amusement soon stopped when they carried on with the jigsaw after dinner. After ten minutes of boredom, Mr Perry stood up, knocked the table and the pieces went flying.

"Oh dear, clumsy me!" he said, bending awkwardly to pick up the pieces strewn everywhere.

Li quickly jumped up to do it. "Don't worry, we'll sort this out."

"You're a good lad," Mr Perry replied.

Whilst the family were busy tidying, Mr Perry discreetly poked Granny in the arm and signalled for her to follow him. That's when she knew he had knocked the table over on purpose! They sneaked out of the kitchen door, through the adjoining back garden gate and into his garage.

"In here," he whispered, opening the door.

He switched on the light and revealed a gleaming, new red mobility scooter!

"Oooh, nice," Granny said, in Chinese.

Mr Perry beamed. "Tonight, me and you," he said, pointing to himself, then Granny, "are going on an AD-VEN-TURE." He mouthed "adventure" slowly, but Granny didn't get it. He showed her his watch, jabbed at the number 12, then pointed at the ground.

It dawned on her – he wanted her to be back there at midnight for a spin on his scooter. YESSSS! Now that was the excitement she wanted!

Granny nodded to let him know she understood, then quickly returned home before anyone noticed she was gone.

Everyone was fast asleep when Granny crept out of bed, fully dressed, and tiptoed out of the house. Mr Perry was already waiting on the scooter. He gave her the thumbs-up and she returned the gesture. She stood on the back of his scooter, clung on to his shoulders and felt a thrill bubbling up inside.

"Ready?" Mr Perry asked.

"Go!" said Granny.

He squeezed the throttle and they trundled off at ten kilometres an hour. They passed several dark streets until a brightly lit building in the distance caught Granny's eye. She prodded Mr Perry and pointed. "There!"

"Aye aye, captain!" he replied, turning right at the traffic lights.

He stopped outside the building and Granny noticed the neon burger sign flickering on the wall. It was a drive-through restaurant! She'd never been to one before.

Mr Perry asked if Granny wanted to eat by pretending to put something in his mouth, then rubbing his belly. She nodded eagerly.

"Two Double Whoopees, please," said Mr Perry, to a metal stand on the roadside. Then he paid and drove the scooter to collect their food from someone at a window – how fascinating! Granny's burger was scrumptious, and she didn't even need chopsticks!

As they were finishing, Mr Perry glanced at his watch.

"Crikey!" he said. Granny guessed by his shocked expression that they'd stayed out too late and should be heading back. They were having such an incredible night, they'd forgotten about the time.

The next morning, Granny was still stuffed from the Double Whoopee burger so she skipped breakfast.

"Are you feeling all right?" asked Li in Chinese, looking worried.

Granny was afraid he'd suspect something so she pretended to have a tummy bug.

"Ah, that's a shame," said Li. "We were going to take you for a drive in the countryside, but if you're not feeling well, we can stay in and finish the jigsaw instead."

ARGH, just Granny's luck! Good job there was another
scooter adventure planned that night — she was getting
tired of that blooming jigsaw!

Granny got to Mr Perry's at midnight and they set off immediately. This time, she told Mr Perry to go left at the traffic lights, which took them through the high street.

All the shops were closed, except one with a flashing sign. Granny's eyes nearly popped out when she figured it might be another burger restaurant, and judging by the long queue outside, the food must be even more delicious than yesterday's.

"There!" Granny cried, eager to try it out.

Mr Perry pulled over.

"What is this place?" he asked the people outside.

"A dance club," a girl answered.

"Oh, I do like a foxtrot, don't you?" Mr Perry said, nudging Granny with his elbow.

She guessed he was asking if she wanted another burger, so of course she nodded. They were let in at the front of the queue, where the doorman gave them a confused look and waved them in.

"We'll show these youngsters what real dancing is all about, won't we, Granny?" said Mr Perry.

Granny didn't understand but he seemed as excited as she was about scoffing another Double Whoopee. When they walked in, Granny noticed no one was eating – they were dancing, because it wasn't a restaurant at all, but a disco, and it looked fantastic!

Mr Perry motioned to Granny for a dance, but she wasn't sure how to. He helped her out by pointing to his feet, balancing her on his toes, then taking her hands. He stepped to the beat, slowly at first, then with big swirling strides.

"We're doing the foxtrot!" shouted Mr Perry.

"Whoo-hoo!" giggled Granny, as a huge crowd gathered to watch.

When they'd finished dancing, everyone cried out for more. But Granny and Mr Perry didn't think it was fair to hog the dance floor all night, so they waved goodbye to their new friends and left for home.

At breakfast, Granny couldn't stop yawning. All that twirling around had exhausted her.

"Oh dear," said Li, in Chinese, looking concerned. "Looks like we might have overdone it with the jigsaw yesterday. We'd better relax with some nice TV nature documentaries today."

ARGH NOOO! How could Granny tell them to stop mollycoddling her without revealing her secret? Maybe she would have to keep playing along and be glad that at least her thrilling nighttime adventures made up for the painfully dull daytimes!

When Granny sneaked over later that night, she was surprised to find Mr Perry packing bags into his scooter basket.

"My turn to choose where we're going," he said, winking.

It looked as if Mr Perry already had plans, so Granny happily let him take charge of directions tonight.
At the traffic lights, they went straight ahead, turned down a bumpy tractor lane and parked in a field. Mr Perry switched on his torch and tipped out a bag full of metal poles and an orange sheet.

"I'm an expert at putting these up," he said. "I was in the army."

All Granny heard was gibberish, but she could see that Mr Perry was building a tent.

Afterwards, he went off to collect some sticks, which Granny knew all about because she'd made hundreds of fires before at her home in China.

"Me, expert," she said, taking over.

When she'd built and lit the fire, Mr Perry applauded her. "I'm impressed, but I bet you've never done *this* before," he said, opening a packet of pink and white balls and squishing one on to the end of a stick. He held it over the fire until it turned golden.

"Marshmallow. Eat," he said with a smile, handing it over. When Granny nibbled it, she was delighted to find that it was sweet, sticky and fluffy, all at the same time – YUM! This was definitely the BEST night so far.

She was about to take another bite when headlights approached. A car parked up and a man and woman in uniform got out.

"Heck, it's the police!"
Mr Perry whispered.

They strode over and the woman
said, "We've had reports of a fire."

Mr Perry whimpered, "It's just
a little one."

"I'm afraid this is private land too,
which means you're trespassing,"
said the man.

None of it made sense to Granny,
but the look on Mr Perry's face told
her they were in trouble.

The man took out his phone and
got ready to dial. "You shouldn't be
out here in the middle of the night.
Do you have anyone we can call to
come and fetch you?"

"No, no, it's fine!" said Mr Perry,
gathering his things in a panic.
"We'll pack up and make our own
way home."

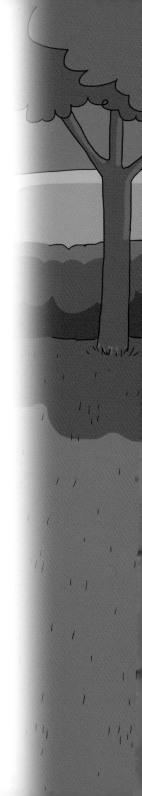

34

The woman nodded. "OK, but we need you gone in ten minutes."

"Of course, Officer," said Mr Perry.

After the police left, they stomped out the fire, rolled up the tent and hurried back home on the scooter.

As they reached the junction, a car Granny recognised went past. It was Li's! He must have noticed she was missing and was out looking for her! Now they really were in trouble.

Granny shook Mr Perry's shoulder. "Is Li!" she hissed, pointing at the car.

Mr Perry gasped. "I'll go the back way," he said, heading in the opposite direction.

They wove through several dark lanes and were almost home, when Li's car suddenly appeared around the corner. Mr Perry hastily attempted a U-turn, but he couldn't turn the scooter quickly enough. They shot straight into a large prickly bush and the wheels just spun as Mr Perry tried to reverse them out. Li stopped his car and jogged over.

"Granny, is that you?" he said.

Phew! He wasn't sure it was her, so there was still a chance she could get away with it. The family mustn't find out she'd been lying the whole time, otherwise they'd put a stop to the only fun she was having on holiday!

"Quick, go!" Granny squealed.

Mr Perry finally managed to reverse, and they escaped. Granny looked over her shoulder – Li was still chasing them. As she turned back, she saw a fox leaping out ahead, forcing Mr Perry to swerve sharply.

They veered straight into a shallow ditch full of water, and Mr Perry groaned as the scooter's battery whirred and died.

When Li finally caught up, he panted, "It *is* you, Granny ... and ... Mr Perry?!"

"We didn't mean to cause any trouble," said Mr Perry, sheepishly.

"We wanted to have fun," Granny winced, in Chinese.

"We were being extra careful because of your age," Li explained.

"But as you can see, I'm sprightlier than you think!" Granny replied.

Then they laughed awkwardly at the misunderstanding.

"I'm just glad you're both safe," said Li. "Let's get you home." He switched to English and added, "We'll sort your scooter out in the morning, Mr Perry."

The next day, Li told everyone what had been going on. Anna looked shocked but the kids were wide-eyed in admiration and seemed a little envious about missing out.

"Does that mean we can do *exciting* stuff now?" said Jack.

"Instead of boring jigsaws and TV?" Luke huffed.

"Well, now we know Granny is a thrill-seeker, why not," said Li. "Any suggestions?"

Jack's face lit up. "Zip lining!" he cried.

"Go-karting!" yelled Luke.

"It's your holiday, Granny, what would you like to do?" said Li, in Chinese.

"Boat ride!" shouted Granny.

She was so relieved her secret was finally out, and that she wouldn't have to secretly sneak out for fun ever again.

"Boat ride, it is!" said Li. "We should invite Mr Perry too, whilst his scooter is being fixed!"

Soon they were all in the car, zooming off for a proper fun-filled day together. The boat ride was spectacular – one of those fast, bumpy ones where everyone got wet – and made Granny laugh until her cheeks were sore!

Each day after that, someone else in the family got to choose an activity and every time it just got better and better. Granny had the time of her life!

Granny had one final request before she returned home to China.

"What's that then?" said Li.

"I'd really love one last ride on Mr Perry's scooter," she begged.

Li frowned for a second and Granny thought she was in trouble again. Then he smirked and replied, "OK ... but only if we can come too!"

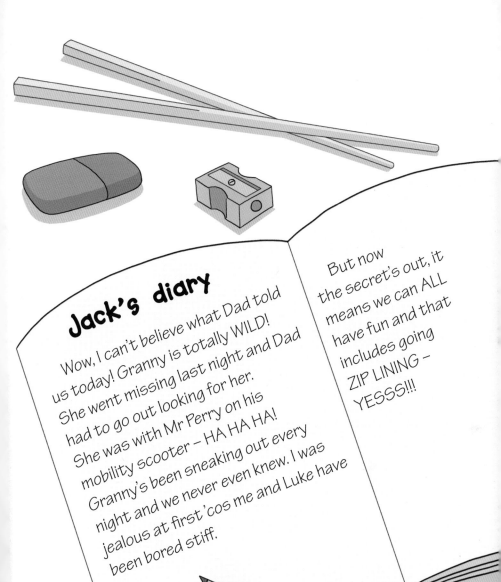

Jack's diary

Wow, I can't believe what Dad told us today! Granny is totally WILD! She went missing last night and Dad had to go out looking for her. She was with Mr Perry on his mobility scooter – HA HA HA! Granny's been sneaking out every night and we never even knew. I was jealous at first 'cos me and Luke have been bored stiff.

But now the secret's out, it means we can ALL have fun and that includes going ZIP LINING – YESSS!!!

 Ideas for reading

Written by Gill Matthews
Primary Literacy Consultant

Reading objectives:

- draw inferences such as inferring characters' feelings, thoughts and motives from their actions, and justifying inferences with evidence
- predict what might happen from details stated and implied
- identify main ideas drawn from more than one paragraph and summarise these

Spoken language objectives:

- articulate and justify answers, arguments and opinions
- give well-structured descriptions, explanations and narratives for different purposes, including for expressing feelings
- use spoken language to develop understanding through speculating, hypothesising, imagining and exploring ideas
- participate in discussions, presentations, performances, role play, improvisations and debates

Curriculum links: Geography: Place knowledge; Locational knowledge

Interest words: capable, raring, sprightlier, thrill-seeker, wild

Resources: IT

Build a context for reading

- Look at the front cover and discuss what the children think is happening. Explore children's understanding of a great granny.
- Read the back cover blurb. Ask children what they think Great Granny Chan is like. Encourage them to support their responses with evidence.
- Look at the title page. Discuss what the children think might happen in the story.

Understand and apply reading strategies

- Read pp2–7 aloud, modelling how to use meaning, punctuation and dialogue to help you read with expression. Explore what children have found out about Granny. Have these pages told them any more about what she is like?